A GUIDE TO NARNIA

100 Questions about
THE CHRONICLES OF NARNIA:
THE LION, THE WITCH AND THE WARDROBE

By the Editors of Catholic Exchange

ASCENSION PRESS

West Chester, PA

Catholic Exchange
Your Faith • Your Life • Your World

Encinitas, CA

Ascension Press
Post Office Box 1990
West Chester, PA 19380
Orders: 1-800-376-0520
www.AscensionPress.com

Cover design: Devin Schadt

Printed in the United States of America

ISBN 1-932645-97-7

Contents

Introduction

C.S. Lewis once remarked that his stories always began with pictures in his head. He pictured floating islands, and eventually, this image became *Perelandra*, the second book in his wonderful Space Trilogy. On another occasion, he pictured a faun, standing under a lamp-post in a snowy wood with an armload of packages, and this image became the inspiration for *The Lion, the Witch and the Wardrobe*, the first in a series of world famous and beloved children's books known as *The Chronicles of Narnia*. *LWW* (as Lewis called it in his letters) was his first foray into a world he would revisit six more times: the magical world of Narnia, a world that bears a striking resemblance to our own.

To be sure, fauns, witches, talking lions and centaurs are in somewhat short supply on this side of the Wardrobe. But sin, evil, betrayal—and faith, honor, and fidelity—are as prevalent as ever, though they're not spoken of as much here as in Narnia. But they still exist, which is why the heart leaps when we enter Narnia. It's not like leaving home and entering a strange world; for us "poor banished children of Eve," it's more like leaving a foreign land and taking a step toward Home. As Professor Digory says in *The Last Battle*, Narnia is "more like the real thing."

A scholar of towering intellect, C.S. Lewis knew that reason mattered, but also that reason alone could not speak to the totality of the human person. A convert to Christianity from atheism, he wrote many books explaining the theology of the Christian faith in lucid prose. But he did more than that. As the Christian tradition had done for centuries, Lewis also told *stories*. In this, he was following his Master, Jesus, who spoke to people not by offering definitions of Justification by Faith and holding seminars on Predestination, the Perspicuity of Scripture, and Modes of Economic Discourse in the Israelite Tradition, but by saying, "There was once a man who had two sons..."

For fifty years the pictures in Lewis' head have been pictures in our heads, too. Pictures by which Christ (who is Himself the "image of the living God" [Hebrews 1:4]) is shown to us. Pictures by which we see not just sin and evil (a staple which modern fiction is too good at portraying), but also characters that embody decency, goodness, courage, virtue, and nobility. We even catch something of the fragrance of Heaven itself. His fiction, and particularly his children's fiction, gives us "drinkable Light."

We live now in a time that is dominated far more by the Image than by the Word. People get their information about life, the universe, and everything else primarily from TV and the movies. People read less and less, and less still do they read works of abstract theology. So the release of *The Lion, the Witch and the Wardrobe* as a motion picture is a particularly welcome event because it gives us the essence of the Gospel in a way that everyone can understand. Still more welcome is the fidelity to the original story the film displays. Through it, the pictures Lewis saw in his mind will become visible to our eyes as well as our minds. And through it, a whole new generation who might have missed this marvelous tale because they are not readers will be introduced to the joys of Narnia and its most gracious

Lord, Aslan. Our prayer is that many will be led from the image on the screen, not merely back to Lewis' words, but to the Word Incarnate, Jesus Christ.

In the movie *Splash*, Tom Hanks' character meets a woman who turns out to be a mermaid. She has no knowledge of our customs here on dry land. So when she is given a present in a gift-wrapped box she exclaims, "How beautiful!" as she admires the box. She has to be prompted to open the present and discover there is much more *inside* the box. Similarly, many moviegoers will receive the story of *LWW* as merely a story and exclaim, "How beautiful!" That's fine by us. But we, the editors of Catholic Exchange and Ascension Press, hope that *A Guide to Narnia—100 Questions about The Chronicles of Narnia: The Lion, the Witch and the Wardrobe* will help Narnia lovers of all ages open the present and discover the riches of Christian truth that Lewis conveys to us through his delightful tale. It's what Father Christmas would want, after all.

— Tom Allen
Editor and President,
CatholicExchange.com
October 19, 2005

CHAPTER I

ABOUT THE CHRONICLES

1) What is *The Lion, the Witch and the Wardrobe*?

The Lion, the Witch and the Wardrobe is the first of the seven *Chronicles of Narnia* written by C.S. Lewis. It is a wonderful story that has entertained children and adults alike for over fifty years. It tells the tale of how Lucy, Edmund, Susan, and Peter Pevensie enter into the land of Narnia through a magic wardrobe and, with the help of the great Lion Aslan, deliver it from the enchantment of the White Witch. It is a story of excitement and adventure, honor and betrayal, good and evil, life and death—and resurrection. The stories, in addition to be being a rollicking good read, portray aspects of Christianity in a way that younger children can understand and adults can profit from as well.

2) Who was C.S. Lewis?

C.S. ("Clive Staples") Lewis (1898–1963) was one of the most famous and widely-read Christian writers of the 20th century. As a child, he and his brother invented the world of "Boxen," a land of talking animals. And as he grew older, he developed a love of fantasy literature, fed in particular by 19th century fantasy writer George MacDonald, whom Lewis referred to as "my master."

As a professor of Medieval and Renaissance literature at England's Oxford and Cambridge Universities,

Lewis wrote many academic works. But he achieved his greatest fame and accomplishment as an apologist for the Christian faith and as a writer of children's novels, science fiction, and fantasy. His thoughtful, everyday explanations of Christianity are still widely read and have helped many understand and deepen their faith.

Born and raised in Belfast, Northern Ireland, Lewis abandoned Christianity as a teenager and declared himself an atheist. After much reading, searching, and the influence of his Oxford friends (including J.R.R. Tolkien, who played a pivotal role in his conversion to faith in Christ), Lewis came to a belief in God and ultimately became a Christian at the age of 33. For the rest of his life, in addition to maintaining his full academic duties, Lewis wrote books on Christian theology and the Christian life that were instrumental in aiding many people to embrace the faith or to come to a more vibrant understanding of it. In *Mere Christianity*, Lewis sought "to explain and defend the belief that has been common to nearly all Christians at all times." Thus Christians of every denomination are able to embrace his clear explanations of the faith.

Lewis' love of fantasy and his towering gifts as a writer of imagination, humor, wisdom, clarity, and beauty can be seen not only in his theological works, but also in his fiction. From *The Screwtape Letters* (a look at human temptation via an imaginary correspondence between a senior devil named Screwtape and his apprentice, Wormwood) to his celebrated "Space Trilogy" (three science fiction novels set on Mars, Venus, and Earth) to *The Great Divorce* (a look at damnation and beatitude via a bus ride from hell to heaven), Lewis has enthralled readers with his wonderful stories for more than sixty years.

In the 1950s, Lewis began writing his most popular books—a series of fantasies for children, collectively known as *The Chronicles of Narnia*. The first book in the series, *The Lion, the Witch and the Wardrobe* proved to be so popular that Lewis began work on six sequels. All told, the seven books of *The Chronicles* have sold 85 million copies worldwide. Christian concepts can be found throughout the stories.

3)   Where is *Narnia*?

Narnia, like Middle Earth of J.R.R. Tolkien's *Lord of the Rings* trilogy, is a fictional world. It is a land filled with talking animals, mythical creatures, and magic.

The geography of Narnia is mostly forest, with hills rising into low mountains in the south and marshlands in the north. To the east of Narnia lies the Eastern Ocean, to the west rises a great mountain range, to the north flows the River Shribble, and to the south lies the land of Calormen.

The Great River is at the center of Narnia, and it flows from the northwest on an east-southeasterly course to the Eastern Ocean. Narnia is ruled from the castle of Cair Paravel, at the mouth of the Great River.

4)   Are *The Chronicles of Narnia* a Christian series?

Yes and no. Although the seven books were not written as explicitly Christian works, the characters and events found within them often reflect Christian themes. As C.S. Lewis himself once remarked, "The whole Narnian story is about Christ. That is to say, I asked myself, 'Supposing that there really was a world like Narnia and supposing it had (like our world) gone wrong and supposing Christ wanted to go into that world and save it (as He did ours) what might have happened?'"

We can see parallels to the Gospel throughout *The Chronicles*. For example, the hero of the series, Aslan the Lion, dies, comes back to life, and ultimately saves Narnia. The author uses the figure of a lion for Jesus because the lion is the king of the animals, and also because the Old Testament refers to the Messiah as the "lion of Judah."

The story of Narnia reflects Christian salvation history: *The Magician's Nephew* deals with creation and the entrance of evil into Narnia; *The Lion, the Witch and the Wardrobe* alludes to the death and resurrection of Jesus; *Prince Caspian* shows how true religion was corrupted and then restored; and *The Last Battle*, the final book, describes how an "Antichrist" character, Shift the Ape, tries to take over Narnia, which leads to Aslan's second coming.

Most children, though, will probably not pick up on much of this symbolism—for them, Narnia is just an exciting story in which heroes win out over villains and good conquers evil in dramatic fashion.

5) **Is there a specific order that one should read *The Chronicles*?**

As we shall see, time in Narnia and time in our world don't always line up. In a funny way, this is reflected in the order of the books. In our world, *The Lion, the Witch and the Wardrobe* was written in 1950. It was followed by the other *Chronicles* in this order:

- *Prince Caspian* (1951)

- *The Voyage of the Dawn Treader* (1952)

- *The Silver Chair* (1953)

- *The Horse and His Boy* (1954)
- *The Magician's Nephew* (1955)
- *The Last Battle* (1956)

However, in terms of Narnian history, the sequence is:

- *The Magician's Nephew*
- *The Lion, the Witch and the Wardrobe*
- *The Horse and His Boy*
- *Prince Caspian*
- *The Voyage of the Dawn Treader*
- *The Silver Chair*
- *The Last Battle*

None of this matters much. As C.S. Lewis states in a 1957 letter written to an American boy named Laurence:

> I think I agree with your order [i.e. chronological] for reading the books more than with your mother's. The series was not planned beforehand as she thinks. When I wrote *The Lion* I did not know I was going to write any more. Then I wrote *P. Caspian* as a sequel and still didn't think there would be any more, and when I had done *The Voyage* I felt quite sure it would be the last. But I found I was wrong. So perhaps it does not matter very much in which order anyone reads them. I'm not even sure that all the others were written in the same order in which they were published. (from *Letters to Children*)

For what it's worth, Walt Disney Pictures and Walden Media chose *The Lion, the Witch and the Wardrobe* as the first of the *Chronicles* to be made into a major motion picture because it was the first one written, and they plan on following up with *Prince Caspian*.

6) Is the movie based on the book?

Yes. According to its producers, the Walt Disney Pictures/Walden Media movie (release date: December 9, 2005) is faithful to the original book. Of course, as with any filmed adaptation of a novel, the screenwriter and director have changed some details to enhance the story's dramatic and visual effect. But the movie essentially portrays the story as C.S. Lewis originally wrote it.

CHAPTER 2

THE STORY BEGINS

---

7) Why are the four children sent to the Professor's house?

Since it is 1940, World War II is raging and German bombs are being dropped on London. For their own protection, the children are sent far from their home in the city to the Professor's large country house. During this dark and dangerous period of history, many English families sent their children out of the cities to stay with relatives living in the countryside.

8) Who is the Professor?

Professor Kirke is Digory, the boy from *The Magician's Nephew*, as an old man. He also appears at the happy ending of *The Last Battle*.

In *The Magician's Nephew*, Digory's uncle makes magic rings that allow their wearers to travel to other worlds by passing through the "Wood between the Worlds." After leaving the Wood and entering another world, Digory gives in to temptation, breaks a magic spell, and releases Jadis (who would become the White Witch) from the dead world, Charn. He accidentally brings her back to London and, ultimately, to Narnia. As a boy, Digory represents the power of free will and its consequences.

9) How old are the children?

The book never tells us any of the children's ages, just that Lucy will be old enough to go to boarding school "next year." Fortunately, though, Lewis wrote out a timeline spanning 2,555 years of Narnian history from which we learn their ages at the time they enter Narnia through the Wardrobe: Lucy turns eight that year; Edmund, ten; Susan, twelve; and Peter, thirteen.

CHAPTER 3

AFTER LUCY GOES THROUGH THE WARDROBE

---

10) Why does Lucy go into the Wardrobe?

One rainy day when the children can't go outside to play, they decide to explore the Professor's large house. They soon come upon a room with nothing in it but a large, wooden wardrobe. While the other three quickly run ahead, Lucy is intrigued and wants to see what is inside, though she thinks it will be locked. When the door opens easily, she goes in and her adventure in Narnia begins, an adventure which will soon involve all of her siblings as well.

11) What makes the Wardrobe magical?

The Wardrobe is magical because it is made of Narnian wood. An explanation of this remarkable fact is found in the first book of the series, *The Magician's Nephew*. Digory, the "nephew" of the story, brought an apple back from Narnia and planted the core in our world. Though the tree grew in our world, its wood was Narnian so it retained its magical power. When the tree was blown down in a storm, the Wardrobe was made from its wood. It served as an entrance into Narnia three times: once for Lucy alone, then for Lucy and Edmund, and finally for all four children.

12) Why couldn't the children experience the magical power of the Wardrobe unless "both feet were in"?

C.S. Lewis probably uses this as a metaphor for being totally committed to a particular path or course of action. In other words, the children cannot experience Narnia by keeping "one foot" in this world—they need to plunge totally into its magic.

Similarly, as Christians, we are called to follow Jesus with our whole hearts, minds, and souls. If we want to experience His grace in our lives and ultimately enter heaven, we must take up our cross daily and follow Him. Jesus has strong words for those who are "lukewarm" or "half-hearted" in their commitment to Him (see Revelation 3:16). If we want to be holy, we can't keep "one foot in" the world; we need to keep both feet firmly planted in the Kingdom of God.

13) What is a lamp-post doing in a forest in Narnia?

In *The Magician's Nephew*, the first book in the *Chronicles*, we read about how Aslan created Narnia and how the lamp-post was grown from a bar that Jadis (the future White Witch) brought from London. It serves as a reference point for the children as they find their way through Narnia, helping point them in the right direction.

We can see how the lamp-post might be a symbol referring to Jesus, "the light of the world." In the light of the Gospel Jesus reveals that we do not stumble in the darkness of our sins but walk in the light of God's truth.

14) Is the lamp-post significant to Christianity?

In Matthew 5.14-16, in the Sermon on the Mount, Jesus tells His disciples: "You are the light of the world. A city set on a hill cannot be hid. Nor do men light a lamp and put it under a bushel, but upon a [lamp] stand, and it gives light to all in the house. Let your light so shine before men, that they may see your good works and give glory to your Father who is in heaven."

The lamp-post is present in the Wild Woods of the West to give light to all who come into Narnia. Several good deeds take place in its light. Mr. Tumnus and Peter ask for Lucy's forgiveness there, and at the end of the four children's time in Narnia, they discuss all of the good they have accomplished and resolve that they must continue together to perform good works and follow the path set before them.

15) Who is the first character Lucy meets in Narnia?

The first Narnian creature Lucy meets is Mr. Tumnus, who is a faun. In Roman mythology, a *faun* is a creature that has the upper body of a man and the horns, ears, tail, and legs of a goat. Fauns live in untamed woodlands and forests. In Greek mythology, a faun is known as a *satyr.*

16) Why does the Faun, Mr. Tumnus, call Lucy a "daughter of Eve"?

We need to remember that none of the creatures in Narnia are human. Although Mr. Tumnus has never seen a human being, he calls Lucy a "daughter of Eve" because she is a girl and he knows that all humans are descendants of Adam and Eve. Also, there is a legend in Narnia that speaks of the "sons of Adam" and the "daughters of Eve."

In the popular devotional prayer *Hail, Holy Queen*, we pray, "To thee do we cry, poor banished children of Eve ..." Our Christian faith teaches that Eve is mother of all the living, so women are her "daughters" and men are her "sons." We are "banished" due to original sin, and we ask Mary's help to resist temptation and grow in holiness.

17) How does Mr. Tumnus entice Lucy to go with him to his home?

Mr. Tumnus entices Lucy to his home by offering her things he knew she would enjoy: warmth from the cold, tea, and cake. While these things are good in and of themselves, Mr. Tumnus intends to use them for a bad end—namely, to hand Lucy over to the White Witch.

In a similar way, the seemingly innocent and harmless things of the world can distract us and ultimately turn us away from doing what is right. If we let ourselves love the world more than God, we will lose sight of our purpose and set ourselves up for trouble.

18) Who is the White Witch?

The White Witch is the chief villain of *The Lion, the Witch and the Wardrobe*. She is an evil creature who stole the throne of Narnia and cast a spell causing it to be "always winter and never Christmas." By the beginning of the book, the winter had lasted 100 years.

We learn in *The Magician's Nephew* that her real name is Jadis, and that her pale white appearance is caused by her eating a forbidden apple from the Emperor's Garden in Narnia at the beginning of that world. Only those who were instructed to take one of these apples could do so, and even then they could not eat it themselves but had to give it to another for their benefit. By eating an apple without permission, Jadis became evil and her skin turned white. Her magical powers flow mostly from her wand, which allows her to turn creatures into stone.

Here we can see a parallel with the creation story in Genesis, specifically the sin of Adam and Eve in eating the forbidden fruit from the tree of the knowledge of good and evil (see Genesis, chapter 3). Their sin condemned them and all their descendents to a life of hard work, suffering, and death, when our bodies return to the dust of the earth (rather like turning to stone). It is only with the passion, death, and resurrection of Jesus that we have been reconciled with God and now have the hope of salvation and eternal life.

So the White Witch's "fall," like that of Satan, confirms her in a life of evil, always grasping at power and domination over the inhabitants of Narnia. She calls herself "Her Imperial Majesty Jadis, Queen of Narnia, Chatelaine of Cair Paravel, and Empress of the Lone Islands." It is also worth noting that, though entirely corrupt, she remains extremely beautiful. This recalls St. Paul's warning that "Satan disguises himself as an angel of light" (2 Corinthians 11:14).

19) Is the Witch human?

No, she's not. But she claims to be so she can rule over Narnia. At the creation of Narnia, Aslan gives "the sons of Adam and the daughters of Eve" the right to rule over all of its animals and magical creatures. By falsely claiming to be a "daughter of Eve," the White Witch can call herself Queen of Narnia.

Despite her unnatural skin color and above-average height, the White Witch *appears* to be human. But she is actually descended from the Jinn (ugly and evil demons having supernatural powers which they can bestow on those who summon them) and the giants. This race once inhabited Charn, a dying world from which Jadis escapes in *The Magician's Nephew*.

20) **Before the winter, we're told that the streams of Narnia flowed with wine rather than water. What is the meaning behind this?**

This is a clear reference to the Gospel of John as well as to any number of pagan myths. At the wedding feast of Cana (see John 2:1-11), Jesus turns water in stone jugs into wine. This is Jesus' first miracle, and with it He begins His public ministry and begins to reveal to the apostles who He is. Likewise, in Greek mythology (which Lewis loved), wine is the symbol of joy, abundance, and plenty, much as it is in the Psalms, as when the Psalmist rejoices "There are many who say, 'O that we might see some good! / Lift up the light of thy countenance upon us, O Lord! / Thou hast put more joy in my heart / than they have when their grain and wine abound'" (Psalm 4:6-7).

Narnia was created by Aslan as an idyllic and magical land, where different creatures live together in happiness and peace. Since wine is a drink of celebration and comfort, it is appropriate that Narnian streams would flow with wine before the winter caused by the wicked rule of the White Witch.

21) What is wrong with the seasons in Narnia after the White Witch takes over?

After the White Witch seizes power and begins her illegitimate rule over Narnia, there is only one season: winter. So life is always cold and dreary, without any hope of the coming of the warmth and brightness of spring.

Theologically, the seasons mirror the cycle of life: the warmth and full bloom of summer can be seen to symbolize life at its full strength and vigor; autumn (or fall) is a reflection of life growing older and slower; the cold of winter, death; and spring, new life.

22) Does the White Witch practice "white magic"?

You may hear some people make a distinction between so-called "white magic," which is used for the benefit of others, and "black magic," which is used to harm others. Because of this, you would think that a "white witch" would be one who practices white magic and is therefore good. In the *Chronicles*, however, "white" refers to snow, ice, and the cold of death. So, far from being good, the White Witch is a destructive force in Narnia. In addition, we are told that the color of the skin on her face and arms is a deathly white.

23) What does the White Witch represent?

She is a representation—a *personification*—of evil. Since she directly opposes Aslan, who is good, and everyone who follows him, she could be said to represent the devil, who desires to turn everyone against their ultimate good—God.

Like the devil, the White Witch's considerable powers are ultimately no match against the forces of good. In the end, she is destroyed by her own evil works.

24) Why doesn't Mr. Tumnus turn Lucy over to the White Witch?

Though he is in the service of the White Witch, Mr. Tumnus regrets this when he comes to see that Lucy, as a daughter of Eve, is good. He decides not to turn her over to the White Witch because he realizes this would be wrong. By making the decision to do what is right, Mr. Tumnus knows he may have to suffer the anger of the Witch and perhaps be turned into stone. Nonetheless, he is willing to risk his very life to see that Lucy gets home safely.

Mr. Tumnus, then, can be said to have had a conversion experience—by failing to hand Lucy over to the Witch, he turns away from serving evil to do a profoundly good deed.

25) Peter, Susan, and Edmund meet up with Lucy after she has been through the Wardrobe and tell her she has only been gone a moment. Why is this?

In Lucy's experience, she spends many hours in Narnia with Mr. Tumnus. So she is very surprised when her siblings insist she has been gone only a moment.

Apparently, time in Narnia does not coincide with time on Earth. One can spend hours (or even years) in Narnia, while no time at all elapses on Earth. But the nature of time in Narnia is apparently flexible; it is not always consistent. We can see this explained in *The Voyage of the Dawn Treader*: "If you went back to Narnia after spending a week here, you might find that a thousand Narnian years had passed, or only a day, or no time at all. You never know till you get there."

CHAPTER 4

AFTER EDMUND GOES THROUGH THE WARDROBE

26) Why can't Edmund find Lucy in the Wardrobe when they are playing hide-and-seek?

At first, Edmund doesn't realize that the Wardrobe is actually an entrance to Narnia. He fully expects Lucy to be hiding behind the coats. So he is very surprised to discover that not only is Lucy *not* in the Wardrobe, but that he has actually stepped into another world.

When she enters into Narnia the second time, Lucy runs directly to Mr. Tumnus' home without knowing that Edmund is following after her. When she gets to Tumnus' cave, Lucy is reassured to hear that the White Witch has done nothing to him for letting her go.

27) Why does Edmund describe the Witch as beautiful?

Because, in her own way, she *is* beautiful. We usually think of evil as being ugly, but the opposite is often true. Sin can be very attractive, beautiful, and enticing; for a time, it can mislead us into thinking that it is actually good. Edmund sees the Witch as beautiful not least because she promises to fulfill his selfish desires.

Sometimes we may suspect—or even know—that a particular desire or behavior is evil, but we still pursue it because it is appealing. We can let our sins blind us. The lesson here is that we must be careful to form our hearts and minds according what God has *revealed* to be good and true in the Bible and the teachings of the Church; we should not allow apparent beauty or instant gratification to lead us astray.

28) What is *Turkish Delight*, the candy Edmund seems to love so much?

Turkish Delight is a candy made of jelly-like cubes flavored with rosewater and covered with powdered sugar. Edmund remarks that the pieces of Turkish Delight the Witch gave him were "sweet and light to the very center." In *The Lion, the Witch and the Wardrobe*, they are symbolic of sin: they are delicious at their first taste, but totally unsatisfying in the end. In fact, consuming too much actually makes Edmund feel sick, yet he still craves more. We can see that Edmund's craving for more leads him to other sins and ultimately to betraying his family.

29) Why does the Witch ask Edmund whether there are other children with him?

Because she is very concerned about her future. As we later see in the story, there is a legend in Narnia that when two sons of Adam and two daughters of Eve sit on the four thrones at Cair Paravel, it will not only be the end of the White Witch's reign but also of her life. We should notice, though, that this prophecy requires the free will of those it concerns to be fulfilled, i.e., Edmund is free to reject the Witch's will, the other children are free to reject their destiny, and all are free to accept or reject Aslan. At the same time, all these free choices are going to be woven together by Aslan to fulfill the prophecy.

30) Why does the Witch tell Edmund he can have all the Turkish Delight he wishes if he brings his brother and sisters to her castle?

Because she wants to capture and kill all of them to keep the prophecy from being fulfilled and thus protect her rule over Narnia. The lesson here is that there are always strings attached to evil and sin—and that the devil is a liar. We may not notice the strings right away, but we always do in the end. At first, everything seems wonderful: Edmund gets a warm drink while it is cold outside and he eats the best Turkish Delight he ever tasted. Once he tastes it and is hooked, he wants more and is willing to do whatever he has to do in order to get what he wants. He is blind to the manipulation the Witch is using to get what she wants. Her manipulation is a twisted parody of the offering Aslan will make of himself, and of the loving response he will ask of his followers as he calls for courage in battle against evil.

31) Why does the Witch then tell Edmund she will crown him as High King? Isn't the Turkish Delight enough to get him to do her bidding?

Smaller sins lead to bigger ones. The Witch, by manipulating Edmund with the promise of being King, is leading him on from mere sins of the flesh to sins of the spirit, especially pride and envy. While the offer of more Turkish Delight might have been enough to get him to do her bidding, she chains his soul more profoundly by offering him more. She knows Edmund is resentful of Peter's role as the oldest, and she plays on this resentment with an offer for him to become ruler over all his siblings and, indeed, all of Narnia. Since we're told that Edmund has a mean streak and a selfish disposition, it is an offer he is too weak to refuse.

In the Witch's two-fold temptation of Edmund—with food and power—we can see a reflection of the devil's temptation of Jesus. In the Gospel, we read that Jesus, in preparation for the start of His public ministry, fasted and prayed for forty days and nights in the desert. So the devil tempts Him to turn stones into bread. Jesus responds by saying "Man does not live by bread alone but by every word that comes from the mouth of God." Then the devil promises Jesus power over all the kingdoms of the world if He falls down and worships him. This in turn reflects the temptation of Adam and Eve. The forbidden fruit has two aspects, it was "good for food" and "a delight to the eyes" (the appeal to appetite) and "was to be desired to make one wise" (the appeal to pride and the sins of the spirit). Jesus' response to Satan gives us a clear example of how we must respond when tempted to evil.

32) Why doesn't Edmund suspect the Witch is on the wrong side, especially after she tells him to keep their conversation about him becoming King a secret and not to believe the negative things he may hear about her?

Edmund lets his selfish wants blind him to the truth about the Witch. He *needs* to convince himself she is good to justify his alliance with her; otherwise, he is knowingly committing himself to doing evil. When we choose to follow our own will rather than God's, we can talk ourselves into believing anything. Scripture refers to this as having a "darkened mind" (Ephesians 4:18). As Lewis puts it in *The Magician's Nephew*, "the trouble about trying to make yourself stupider than you really are is that you very often succeed."

In the Garden of Eden, the serpent (representing the devil) tricks Eve by telling her that God doesn't want them to eat from the tree of the knowledge of good and evil because then they would be like God. She was being tempted, and gave in to the serpent's lies. With her encouragement, Adam too sinned by eating the forbidden fruit. Remember—both of them had heard the voice of God Himself and enjoyed His friendship. Even so, they disobeyed His commands out of pride. We too can be easily tricked by the devil into doing what is wrong if we do not listen to God's word and pray for the grace to follow His will in our lives.

33) Why is Edmund so mean to Lucy?

From the beginning of the story, Edmund is portrayed as having a negative attitude and temperament. Peter mentions that he has been "beastly" to the smaller kids at school. He is also negative about the weather when they first get to the Professor's home and it is raining outside. Then he continues to pick on Lucy after she returns from her first visit to Narnia and tells her story to the others. It seems Edmund has a tendency to want attention and power, so maybe he is jealous of Lucy's purity and innocence. Since she embodies what is good, Edmund probably feels a little uncomfortable being around her and so treats her badly. We should note, though, that these are all choices on Edmund's part. He is not "made that way." He *chooses* to be that way. And his bad choices lead to bigger choices with more serious consequences.

34) Edmund hides the fact he has gone through the Wardrobe from his siblings. Why does he do this?

He does this so he can manipulate Peter, Susan, and Lucy into going to the Queen's home once they all get to Narnia. If he says that he has been to Narnia already, then he admits to Peter and Susan that Lucy is right, and he is afraid that her stories about the Witch may sway Peter and Susan into not believing and following him once they are all in Narnia. For his own selfish reasons he does not tell the truth.

35) How does the Professor understand all about the nature of the world of Narnia?

The Professor knows much about Narnia's magic and mystery because he was the first Son of Adam—the first human boy—to go to Narnia. At the end of the story, Aslan allowed Digory to take an Apple of Life back to his world to heal his mother from her terminal illness. After his mother ate the apple and was miraculously cured, Digory took the core and planted it in his garden. The core eventually grew into a great tree that bore the finest apples in England—and still contained the Narnian magic. When Digory was a middle-aged man (and a distinguished professor), it was blown down by a powerful storm. Not wanting it to be chopped up for firewood, the Professor had the Wardrobe made from its wood.

36) The Professor doesn't say much, but when Peter and Susan go and see him about Lucy, he addresses them very seriously. How does he answer their doubts about Lucy and her story about Narnia?

The Professor tells the children there are only three possibilities: Lucy is either lying, "mad" (i.e., crazy), or telling the truth. Since there is no evidence of the first two possibilities, the Professor advises the children to consider the possibility that Lucy is speaking the truth.

Lewis, in his book *Mere Christianity*, makes a similar point about Jesus:

> A man who was merely a man and said the sort of things Jesus said would not be a great moral teacher. He would either be a lunatic—on the level with the man who says he is a poached egg—or else he would be the devil of Hell. You must make your choice. Either this man was and is, the Son of God: or else a madman or something worse. You can shut Him up for a fool, you can spit at Him and kill Him as a demon; or you can fall at His feet and call Him Lord and God. But let us not come with any patronizing nonsense about His being a great human teacher. He has not left that open to us. He did not intend to.

CHAPTER 5

ONCE ALL FOUR CHILDREN HAVE ENTERED NARNIA

37) What effect does sin and selfishness have on Edmund?

Time and time again, Edmund is shown the truth but fails to accept it. When Lucy tells him that a mean witch has caused it to be winter in Narnia (and banished the joyful celebration of Christmas), Edmund tries to convince her that maybe Mr. Tumnus is on the wrong side and that the Witch really is the true Queen of Narnia. Once all four children enter Narnia, Edmund pretends that he has never been there. But he is caught in his lie when he mentions going toward the lamp-post, and he gets angry with Peter for putting Lucy in charge. The lesson here is that selfishness and sin traps Edmund into denying the truth that lies right before his eyes. Sin leads to deeper sin.

38) Isn't Edmund like Judas, the apostle who betrayed Jesus?

It seems Edmund's actions are very similar to Judas' betrayal of Jesus. In the New Testament, we see that Judas only thinks of himself and what he will get in return for turning Jesus over to the authorities—thirty silver coins. We are told that, as keeper of the apostles' funds, he was greedy and often took some of the money for his own use (see John 12:6).

Like Judas, Edmund knows deep in his heart that betraying the others is wrong. But the thought of being King and the promise of more Turkish Delight seems to make his actions worthwhile. When Edmund denies to Peter and Susan that he has been to Narnia, he is thinking only of himself and his own selfish desires. He does this to trick them, so that when all four of them enter Narnia, they will follow him to the Witch's castle so he can have more Turkish Delight and be made King.

Neither Judas nor Edmund think of the long term consequences of their actions or of whom they may hurt. They convince themselves that their own needs are more important than those of others. Sin has blinded them to the truth.

39) How is Mr. Tumnus' behavior Christ-like?

When Mr. Tumnus meets Lucy and realizes that his service to the Witch is wrong, he is willing to sacrifice his own life for Lucy to do the right thing. Lucy knows he had put his life on the line for her, and she in turn wants to help him in any way she can and to save him from the Witch's evil plans. As members of the Church, the body of Christ, we are called to love our neighbor as ourselves.

40) The children know that they should help rescue Mr. Tumnus from the hands of the Witch. Why do they believe this?

The four children know they must help Mr. Tumnus since he helped save Lucy and gets her home safely. He helped their sister and now he needs their help. Our Christian faith teaches us that we are to help all people in need, because all are our brothers and sisters. We are called to do good to others and offer our help to those in need regardless of whether it is inconvenient, uncomfortable, or even dangerous to ourselves.

41) All four children have a strong emotional reaction to hearing the name *Aslan* for the first time. Why is this?

As we're told in the story, when the children hear Mr. Beaver speak Aslan's name, "each of [them] felt something jump on the inside." Each experiences something slightly different: Peter feels brave; Susan, a sensation of a "delicious smell" or "delightful music"; and Lucy has a feeling like the "beginning of the holidays" or summer. On some deep level, they perceive that Aslan (whom they've never met nor know anything about at that point) will set things right in Narnia.

Edmund, though, by putting himself at the service of the White Witch, has sided with evil. Since Aslan is the personification of all that is good and true, Edmund, as a result of his sin, feels uneasy and a little afraid at the mention of Aslan. The conflict shows on his face: he knows he is choosing evil, but he remains determined to serve his own desires.

42) Who is Aslan?

Aslan is "the Lion, the great Lion." He is majestic in appearance, and his presence inspires awe, devotion, joy, and fear all at the same time. He is "Good, but he's not Safe." He is the Creator of Narnia who sang the world into being in the depths of time (as we learn in *The Magician's Nephew*) and he is likewise the one who will undo the Deep Magic from the Dawn of Time (which requires that blood be shed for sin committed) by the sacrifice of himself (which will cause the even

Deeper Magic from Before the Dawn of Time to make death work backward). Those who reject what is good and embrace what is evil are filled with awe, deep hostility, and dread at his presence.

As ruler of Narnia and son of its God, Aslan has to be an animal rather than a human being because Narnia is populated by non-human creatures. He is portrayed as a lion because the lion is the King of the Beasts.

43) What are some of Aslan's titles?

Aslan is called "King of the Wood, Lord of the Whole Wood, King of the Beasts, and King Above all High Kings." He is the "Son of the Great Emperor-beyond-the-Sea"; the great Lion. Aslan assures Lucy that she will have his continued presence when she gets to know him by his earthly name.

As an Oxford tutor and a scholar, C.S. Lewis chose the name *Aslan* because he knew it is the Turkish word for *lion*. Also, *As* is an old Scandinavian word meaning *god*, which Lewis may have known.

44) Who is the Emperor?

The Emperor-beyond-the-Sea (also shortened to just *The Emperor*) is Aslan's father, and it is his declaration of the Deep Magic and the Deeper Magic that Aslan is unwilling—in fact, is unable—to contradict since it is the Law which he himself has established.

When Susan asks if there is anything he can do to save Edmund by going against the Deep Magic, he frowns at her and says: "Work against the Emperor's Magic?" Working against the Emperor's magic would be akin to rebelling against the Emperor himself. Aslan's response to Susan is reminiscent of Jesus' rebuke to St.

Peter—"Get behind me, Satan!"—when Peter suggests He not undergo His passion and death. It also recalls Jesus' words about the Law of Moses: "Think not that I have come to abolish the law and the prophets; I have come not to abolish them but to fulfill them" (Matthew 5:17). The Emperor represents God the Father.

45) What does the White Witch mean by calling herself Empress?

By assuming the title "Empress," the Witch intends to focus all her powers on conquering Aslan, assuming his place, and making herself equal to the Emperor. In her pride, she has deluded herself into believing she can defeat Aslan and continue her terrifying reign over Narnia.

In a similar way, Satan and the other fallen angels (or "demons") sinned in their pride by rebelling against God. As a result, they were cast out of heaven and now seek to tempt us to join their rebellion against God by leading us to sin. We must always strive to live in God's grace by following His teachings in the Bible and the Church, by receiving the sacraments, and by praying that His will be done in our lives.

46) Why is the White Witch evil?

Her selfish desires and her lust for power have blinded her to the good. In *The Magician's Nephew*, we learn that she chose to eat the forbidden apple, thus confirming her in her course of rebellion against the Emperor and his son, Aslan. She is determined to do away with the four children because Narnian prophecy states that four humans will sit on the four thrones of Cair Paravel and rule over Narnia. Having seared her conscience in her pride, she will do anything to accomplish her ends. Ultimately, she is destroyed by her own evil deeds.

47) Why does the White Witch hate Aslan so much?

Because she has fully embraced evil, she cannot stand to be in the presence of good. She is a slave to what Lewis calls "the Great Sin"—namely, the sin of pride. As he says in *Mere Christianity*: "It was through Pride that the devil became the devil: Pride leads to every other vice: it is the complete anti-God state of mind."

Aslan represents all that is good, true, and holy—he is Goodness itself and Love itself. Pride, by contrast, is enmity, as Lewis points out in *Mere Christianity*:

> Pride is essentially competitive—is competitive by its very nature—while the other vices are competitive only, so to speak, by accident. Pride gets no pleasure out of having something, only out of having more of it than the next man. We say that people are proud of being rich, or clever, or good-looking, but they are not. They are proud of being richer, or cleverer, or better-looking than others. If everyone else became equally rich, or clever, or good-looking there would be nothing to be proud about. It is the comparison that makes you proud: the pleasure of being above the rest. Once the element of competition has gone, pride has gone. That is why I say that Pride is essentially competitive in a way the other vices are not.

So it is understandable that she would hate Aslan and all he stands for. He is a threat to her own power and ambition.

We can see this in our own experience. People who are enmeshed in a life of sin often feel uneasy in the presence of holy men and women. Since they are far from the good, they perceive the holy as a burden, and even hearing others speak about God, Jesus, or the teachings of the Church is difficult for them to bear.

Chapter 6

Before Edmund Goes to See the Witch

48) Do all the animals in Narnia talk?

Remember—Narnia is a magical place. Many of its animals have an understanding of human language. Some of them, like Mr. Tumnus and the Beavers, also have the ability to speak themselves. So, although not all creatures in Narnia use words, their communication with the children can be observed (such as when the robin leads them through the woods to the Beavers by flying from tree to tree).

49) How many times does Edmund betray his family?

Three times. The first occasion is when he returns from his first trip to Narnia through the Wardrobe and yet denies to Susan and Peter that he had been there or even that such a place exists.

Next, he denies to Peter that the Witch is evil when they are walking from Mr. Tumnus' home to the Beaver's house. He tries to trick Peter into thinking that maybe Mr. Beaver is bad and the Witch is good, and then asks Peter if he knows the way back home.

Finally, the greatest betrayal of all comes when he learns that the Beavers and his siblings are set to meet Aslan and defeat the Witch. He secretly slips out of the

Beavers' home and runs toward the house of the Witch to report everything he has learned. All this he does out of his own selfish desires—i.e., for more Turkish Delight and to be made King.

These three acts of betrayal may recall for us the three denials of Christ by St. Peter (see Matthew 26:69-75).

50) At what point is there no turning back for Edmund?

This can be seen during Edmund's "betrayal walk" from the Beaver's home to the Witch's castle. He expresses his negative feelings towards Aslan and focuses on what the Witch will show him when they meet. His reaction when Mr. Beaver first mentions Aslan shows that he feels uneasy about the course of action he has decided upon. But his deep-rooted selfishness still drives him to follow the path of sin. He keeps letting himself be tricked by temptation; he tells himself that Peter drove him into leaving, helping him believe he is doing the right thing by going to the Witch.

51) Why does Edmund run away from his siblings and the Beavers?

Edmund wants to get to the Witch's house as soon as possible so he could have more Turkish Delight and be made King of Narnia. This is despite the fact that doing so will likely end up hurting his siblings and himself as well.

This is the true nature of sin: it harms the person who commits it as well as everyone around them. God does not forbid certain actions to spoil our fun and make our lives difficult. Rather, since He truly loves us and wants what is best for us, He forbids certain things because He knows they are harmful to us, being contrary to our nature as human beings, and will only make us unhappy in the end.

52) Is it significant that Edmund commits his final betrayal after having supper with his siblings and the Beavers?

Edmund has been trying to plot when he would betray his family and leave the Beavers during their whole journey in Narnia. Similarly, Judas also betrays Jesus and the apostles out of his own selfish desires. He, too, was looking for the best opportunity to betray his Master. Like Judas at the Last Supper, Edmund betrays his family after their supper with the Beavers.

53) Who is Father Christmas? Could you explain the gifts he gives to the children?

Father Christmas is, of course, the British name for Santa Claus or St. Nicholas. As a legendary figure, Father Christmas is associated with the wonderment of the coming of the Messiah. He embodies the joy of giving and is a symbol of hope to the inhabitants of Narnia, who have endured one hundred dreary years of winter without ever celebrating Christmas.

Instead of giving the children the usual Christmas toys, he gives them practical gifts that will help them during their time in Narnia. They are "survival gifts" to help achieve what they are seeking. Here, Father Christmas seems to be acting as an agent of Aslan (and, by extension, of the Emperor), just as saints do. Interestingly, the gifts he gives are not only useful but reflect something of the true nature of those who receive them. They show something of who Peter, Susan, and Lucy truly are.

Similarly, in prayer and in sacraments such as baptism and confirmation, we receive the gift of God's grace to guide and strengthen us to do His will. Like the children in our story, God gives to each of us exactly what we need to carry out His purpose for our lives. In carrying out that will, Jesus reveals not only God to man, but man to himself.

54) What specifically does Father Christmas give each of the children and why?

To Peter, the oldest, he gives a sword and a shield and tells him that he will use them soon. The shield has a red lion on it, symbolizing that blood will be shed and that Peter will fight for Aslan and his army. Both the sword and the shield are just the right size and weight; they fit him perfectly, and will be used well.

To Susan, he gives a bow, a quiver of arrows, and an ivory horn. He tells her that the bow won't easily miss and that the horn, when blown, will bring help in times of danger. When the wolf attacks, the horn lets Aslan and Peter know that Susan and the others are in danger.

To Lucy, he gives a little bottle containing the juice of the fire flowers that grow on the mountains of the sun. A drop of this liquid is able to heal anyone who is injured or ill. Father Christmas also gives her a small dagger to defend herself in times of great need.

CHAPTER 7

The Children Meet Aslan

55) Isn't it sometimes difficult to turn away from our sins? How is this seen with Edmund?

Yes, it's not always easy to leave our sins behind and walk the path of virtue. We can see this in Narnia when Edmund finally realizes that the Witch is truly evil and that she does not really care about his well-being. The path he travels to this realization, though, is a rough one: he is cold as they travel to the Stone Table; he is hit by the Witch when he tries to defend the fox and the others who were having a party in the forest; the Witch orders her servant to tie his arms and pull him along as they travel rapidly through the forest (he keeps falling and has trouble keeping up); and he would have lost his life if Aslan's army had not come to his rescue.

56) What season follows winter in Narnia? What is significant about this season?

The darkness and cold of the never-ending winter finally turns into the light and warmth of spring, the season of new life, of resurrection. The arrival of spring—coinciding with the arrival of Aslan—signals the end of her treacherous reign and heralds a new beginning for the inhabitants of Narnia.

57) In the book, the sleigh (or sledge) of the Witch is pulled by reindeer. Why are polar bears used in the movie?

This may have been a creative decision of the filmmakers to make a clear visual contrast between the arrivals of the Witch and Father Christmas. In the book the reader can grasp the differences between the jingling arrival of the sleigh of Father Christmas and that of the Witch. The movie, on the other hand, needs to evoke from the audience an immediate horror and fear of the Witch upon her first arrival. Since reindeer have been associated in the popular mind with Christmas, the filmmakers probably chose to have the Witch's sleigh pulled by bears to keep the visual impact unmistakable and in no way misleading.

58) In Narnia, some animals and creatures are good while others are bad because they are allied with the White Witch. Who are the Witch's allies?

The White Witch calls many creatures to do battle against Aslan, including:

- *giants*

- *werewolves*

- *the spirits of evil trees and poisonous plants*

- *the people of the toadstools*

- *boggles* (a small, grotesque supernatural creature that makes trouble for humans; can evoke feelings of dread and apprehension; also known as *hobgoblins* or *bogeys*)

- *ogres* (in fairy tales and legends, an ugly giant that eats human beings)

- *minotaurs* (in Greek mythology, a monster that had the head of a bull and the body of a man; killed young men and women who were sacrificed to him in the labyrinth where he lived on the island of Crete)

- *incubuses* (in Western Medieval legend, a demon that assaults people while they are sleeping; from the Latin *incubare*, "to lie upon")

- *spectres* (a phantom, appartition, or ghost)

- *wraiths* (an apparition of a person who is still alive, seen as a sign or omen that the person is about to die; also used as another word for "ghost")

- *efreets* (a powerful evil spirit or, in Arabic mythology, a gigantic and monstrous demon)

- *ettins* (an ancient name for a giant; originally meant "gluttonous"— i.e., one who eats too much—which tends to make one large)

59) Why does the Wolf deserve a name and title?

Most Narnian creatures are referred to by their animal name only. But the particular wolf that guards the entrance to the Witch's castle and does her deadly bidding is called *Maugrim* (or *Fenris Ulf* in older American editions of the book). He holds the title "Captain of the Secret Police."

Why does the author give such special attention to him? One reason is that all the Narnian animals are placed according to the human traits given them in fairy tales, myths, and legends. In such stories, wolves are typically portrayed as being treacherous, vicious, spiteful, and totally lacking in mercy (see *Aesop's Fables*). Given this, we can see why C.S. Lewis would assign him to the task of being right-hand "man" to the Witch; he has the perfect temperament to carry out her evil designs.

In his works, Lewis uses imagery from 20th century totalitarian governments. We don't normally hear of the "secret police" in old fairy tales. But Lewis thought that for all its many shortcomings in terms of living up the Gospel, the 20th century had excelled at one thing: it showed us better than any other age what Hell was like. Accordingly, he introduces *The Screwtape Letters* by remarking:

> [We] live in the Managerial Age, in a world of "Admin." The greatest evil is not now done in those sordid "dens of crime" that Dickens loved to paint. It is not done even in concentration camps and labour camps. In those we see its final result. But it is conceived and ordered (moved, seconded, carried and minuted) in clean, carpeted, warmed, and well-lighted offices, by quiet men with white collars and cut fingernails and smooth-shaven cheeks who do not need to raise their voice. Hence naturally enough, my symbol for Hell is something like the bureaucracy of a police state or the offices of a thoroughly nasty business concern.

We can see something like Screwtape's hellish police state present in the regime of the Witch.

60) Which Narnian creatures are on Aslan's side?

When the children first meet Aslan, he is accompanied by naiads, dryads, centaurs, a unicorn, a bull, a pelican, an eagle, a great dog, and two leopards. All these creatures come from Greek mythology and medieval heraldry. Many of them symbolize various virtues—the unicorn symbolizes purity; the pelican, sacrificial love; the eagle, vision; the dog, fidelity; and the leopard, swiftness. Those animals that had been turned to stone by the White Witch and freed from their prisons by the breath of Aslan include dwarfs, horses, giants, lions, other centaurs, unicorns, eagles, and dogs. They join his army and help fight against the forces of the Witch.

61) What are *naiads* and *dryads*?

They are female spirit creatures from Greek and Roman mythology. *Naiads* are water nymphs that live in rivers, brooks, springs, and fountains. *Dryads* are wood nymphs who live and die with the trees of which they are the spirits. Their physical appearance reflects the type of tree they live in. Dryads like to dance and are mentioned in the *Chronicles* as the dancing partners of fauns.

In Lewis' world, the figures from pagan mythology who side with Aslan represent the natural human joys and virtues which are meant to find fulfillment in Christ. They also represent Nature, submissive in love to the rightful authority of her Master and Creator, God. They further image the fact that creation is good, not a merely neutral collection of atoms and energy. As St. Paul says, "the whole creation has been groaning in travail together until now" awaiting the day when "creation itself will be set free from its bondage to decay and obtain the glorious liberty of the children of God" (Romans 8:21-22).

62) **When scuffling over who will approach Aslan first, why does Mr. Beaver say to Peter, "Sons of Adam before animals"?**

Mr. Beaver realizes that humans rank higher than animals. His expression is akin to saying "women and children first" in a disaster. According to Narnian prophecy, four humans would come into the land and break the power of the White Witch. They would rule over Narnia with justice from four thrones in Cair Paravel. So the Beaver understands it is far more important to save the children from the Witch than it is to save himself or his family. In addition, by saying "Sons of Adam before animals" he is instructing Peter and the other children of their importance to the future of Narnia. This is reflective of the teaching of Genesis 1 and 2 that human beings, made in the image and likeness of God, have dominion over creation and over the creatures of the earth.

63) **Explain the discussion between the Witch and her Dwarf about the four thrones at Cair Paravel.**

While they were holding Edmund captive, the Witch and the Dwarf figure that if only three of the thrones are filled, the prophecy would not be fulfilled and the Witch would not lose her life. While the Dwarf recommends they keep Edmund alive as a bargaining chip with Aslan, the Witch recognizes that there is a great danger he would be rescued. Thus they decide to kill him immediately.

64) **Why does the Witch say the Stone Table is the proper place to kill Edmund?**

The mysterious, deeply-carved inscription on the Stone Table calls for the sacrifice of traitors. Since

Edmund is clearly a traitor to Aslan and his siblings, the Witch rightly believes that the Stone Table would be the proper place for his death. The Stone Table represents, in part, the Law. Lewis has in mind here both the Natural Law that enlightens human conscience and the revealed Law of Moses. We know this because Lewis speaks of the Law written on the Table in ways which link it not only to the Emperor's sceptre (symbolizing revealed truth) but with the "World Ash Tree" (an image borrowed from pagan Norse mythology). His point is that the Moral Law is knowable to all, not just to Jews and Christians. It speaks with unbreakable authority saying certain things are wrong and must be punished, just as certain things are right and must be rewarded. The Law is unbreakable. Even Aslan himself cannot break it without causing Narnia to be overturned and perish in fire and water.

65) When does Edmund realize he is going to be killed?

In the book, when Edmund is exhausted from the night ride and long walk, he realizes that the Witch intends to kill him only when she and the Dwarf settle on his fate and the Dwarf ties him to a tree.

66) How is Edmund rescued in the book?

Just as the dwarf was about to cut Edmund's throat, the Witch and the Dwarf are attacked by centaurs, unicorns, deer, and birds. The Witch immediately turns herself into a boulder and the Dwarf into an old tree stump. Disguised, they escape notice. Their attackers, having rescued Edmund, soon leave.

67) Why does Peter receive the title "Sir Peter Wolf's-Bane"?

The word *bane* means to be the cause of fatal injury or ruin, so Peter is recognized as the Wolf's worst enemy when he kills Maugrim in battle.

68) How does Aslan treat Edmund upon his safe return to Aslan and his army?

Much like Jesus would have done, Aslan takes Edmund aside and speaks with him privately for a while. He realizes Edmund is truly sorry for his betrayal and is willing to set things right. Aslan even tells Peter, Susan, and Lucy not to talk about it with him. He says this not because it should be forgotten, but because he has forgiven him and Edmund is truly sorry.

69) Please explain how Edmund is forgiven.

Lewis repeatedly stresses the significance of forgiveness and the effect it has on both the person who is asking for forgiveness and the person being forgiven. Mr. Tumnus, after trying to trick Lucy into falling asleep in his home, asks if she can forgive him and she does so willingly and lovingly. At the beginning, you see the hurt it causes Lucy when Edmund asks for forgiveness about not believing in Narnia, and then turns his back and lies to Susan and Peter about it. Later, Peter asks for Lucy's forgiveness when he finds out that Narnia does in fact exist. Then Aslan forgives Edmund for his ultimate betrayal and so do his siblings, which helps bring Edmund back to his old self again and renews his ties with his family. Here Lewis is clearly trying to show that Jesus teaches us that asking for forgiveness when we are truly sorry and forgiving those who are sorry, are the right things to do. In fact, he tells us that if we will not forgive others, we shall not be forgiven (Mark 11:25).

CHAPTER 8

ASLAN, THE WITCH AND REDEMPTION

---

70) Why does Aslan bargain with the Witch?

Aslan offers the Witch a target even more tempting than Edmund's life: his own. Like Jesus, Aslan puts himself in a position where (it would seem) the devil can have the ultimate victory by killing God himself. He offers his life freely for Edmund's, despite the fact that Edmund, so far from deserving such a sacrifice, is actually worthy of death. The Witch, in her hatred of Aslan, likewise freely takes the bait in the hope of destroying Aslan once and for all, and with the intention of afterward destroying the children as well and placing all of Narnia forever in her grip.

71) What do Aslan and Father Christmas prepare Peter for?

Aslan and Father Christmas prepare Peter for the impending great battle against the White Witch and her allies. Father Christmas gives him the sword and shield for fighting, and Aslan tells him what he must do. Like St. Peter in the Bible, to whom Jesus gives authority to lead the apostles (see Matthew 16:18-19), he must use the tools Father Christmas and Aslan have given him if he is to fulfill his destiny.

72) Is there any significance to Peter's name?

His name is from a Greek word meaning "rock," and this shows his strength and character. As the oldest, his siblings look up to him and rely upon him to make the important decisions. Ultimately, he is to be more than just the "rock" for his brother and sisters, but for all of Narnia as well.

After killing the Wolf and fighting with Aslan's forces in the Great Battle against the Witch, he is eventually crowned High King. Similar to the apostle Peter, he plays an important role of leading the "good army" to victory and it is he who Aslan talks to the most about leading his people. Similarly, he reigns with another king and two queens as the "first among equals" just as St. Peter was the Chief of the Apostles yet the servant of all.

73) When Aslan tells Peter he may not be there physically with him for the battle so he must listen and act, what is he trying to do?

He wants Peter to be prepared and to know that with Aslan's guidance, he can fight physically by himself because Aslan is with him. Jesus equips us with what we need too, and we must trust Him, like Peter must trust Aslan. He may not be able to be with us physically, but He is always with us. When He rose to heaven in front of the twelve apostles, although he was not with them physically, He remained with them by sending the Holy Spirit. He calls us to act in obedience to him in order to grow in grace and in the strength of the Holy Spirit. So, as St. Paul tells us in Philippians 2:12-13, "work out your own salvation with fear and trembling" (which, as Lewis observed, makes it sound as though *we* are to do everything) "for God is at work in you, both to will and to work for his good pleasure" (which, as Lewis also observed, makes it sound as though *God* is doing everything). So Peter acts freely, using all the gifts Aslan has given him. It is he who wins the battle, yet it is only by Aslan's power that he does so.

74) Why can't the White Witch look directly into Aslan's eyes?

The White Witch knows Aslan is more powerful than she, but she can't resist confronting and trying to conquer him. She deludes herself into thinking that she just needs to figure out how. The Witch, having committed herself to evil, cannot endure being in the presence of good. Evil, a parasite upon good and dependent on it for existence, can never bear to face true Goodness.

75) What does Aslan mean by "his offense was not against you," when speaking to the Witch about Edmund?

Throughout the story, Edmund is serving his pride and gluttony. He repeatedly and deliberately chooses to do anything necessary—however evil—to satisfy his desires. It's not that he chooses to ally himself with the Witch for her sake. Rather, he only wants what she promises to give him.

Most people don't sin because they deliberately seek to align themselves with evil. Rather, they allow themselves to fall into sin because of some "good" they want: power, pleasure, money, etc. As fallen human beings, we can easily delude ourselves into thinking something bad is really good simply to satisfy our own desires. If anything, Edmund has sought to serve the

Witch, not harm her. Aslan's point is that her claim on Edmund's life is, like everything else, rooted in a lie. She herself has tempted him to be a traitor. She therefore has a claim on his blood, but it is a lie that his offense is againts her. In truth, he has offended Aslan, who is willing to offer his life for Edmund nonetheless.

76) How can Edmund be unaware of the Witch's presence when she and Aslan meet?

Although no one hears Aslan's talk with Edmund, it is remarkable how after their walk, Edmund keeps his gaze directed upon Aslan. By resting his eyes only on the Lion, we can see that he has freely and without reservation chosen to follow the Good. By not even giving evil (in the form of the Witch) a glance, it appears he has had a true conversion experience. He will probably not allow himself to be drawn into sin again. His goal is not to fight the evil of the Witch with his own strength (which is simply another form of pride), but to love Aslan and trust him.

As Christians, we commit ourselves to following God's will in our lives. As such, we should pay no attention to the temptations the devil throws our way; we should always keep our eyes fixed on God and His loving plan.

77) What is the Stone Table?

The Stone Table is a large slab of grey stone, supported by four upright pillars of stone. As we have already seen, it partly symbolizes the Moral Law. But there is more to the Stone Table. For it is also a place upon which sacrifice is made. The White Witch states that the Stone Table is the proper place for killing and the place where killing has always been done.

Although its size is not mentioned in the book, it would need to be low in height because the two girls are able to kneel and still kiss Aslan's face as he lies on top of it. Unknown to the White Witch, it was decreed before the beginning of time that the Table would crack when an innocent victim was willingly killed in the place of a traitor, and death would work backwards. This is exactly the circumstances of Aslan's self-sacrifice on behalf of Edmund. As soon as the sun comes up in Narnia following the death of Aslan, the Table immediately breaks in half with a loud noise and the Risen Lion appears to the girls.

78) What does the Stone Table represent?

We can see that the Stone Table closely resembles an *altar*. In the Old Testament, God commanded his chosen people, the Israelites, to offer Him animal sacrifices on an altar in atonement for their sins. The Church has celebrated the Holy Eucharist on an altar from the very beginning. Our Catholic faith teaches that the Eucharist is the *re-presentation* of the sacrifice of Jesus on the Cross, and the bread and wine truly become the body and blood of Christ.

79) Why does the Witch claim Edmund belongs to her?

The Witch maintains that the inscription on the Stone Table (the Deep Magic) makes the Edmund hers because he is a traitor. As she says, "His life is forfeit to me. His blood is my property." She explains her rights according to the Deep Magic. "[Aslan] knows that unless I have blood as the Law says all Narnia will be overturned and perish in fire and water." With these words, the Witch is merely affirming the order of things as set down by the Emperor, an order that must be followed or the very foundation of Narnia would be destroyed.

80) What is the Deep Magic?

The Deep Magic is written on the Stone Table and is engraved on the sceptre of the Emperor-beyond-the-Sea. It says that every traitor belongs to the White Witch as her lawful prey, and that for every treachery she has a right to exact the ultimate punishment—death.

Here we can see a parallel between the "Deep Magic" in Narnia and the Moral Law, expressed in the Ten Commandments of the Old Testament. With the original sin of Adam and Eve, mankind fell into a state of sin, suffering, and death. In a sense, we became slaves of the devil—just as Edmund could be said to be a slave of the White Witch. God, in His great love and mercy, offers salvation to humanity, first by putting the Natural Law into the hearts of all, then by choosing a people—the Israelites—to whom He reveals His law of life. In this Law, God decrees that His people must offer the sacrifice of animals in atonement for their sins. These sacrifices would last until the ultimate sacrifice for sin, the passion, death, and resurrection of Jesus, would definitively end the reign of sin and bring about the Kingdom of God.

81) What is "the Magic that is Deeper than the Deep Magic"?

We're told that the Deep Magic traces only to the dawn of time. But, a little further back, before time dawned,

there was a different incantation: the "Deeper Magic."
This decree of the Emperor states that when a willing
victim who had committed no treachery—i.e., one who
is totally innocent—is killed in a traitor's stead, the
Stone Table would crack and Death itself would start
working backwards. This incantation was unknown
to the White Witch, so she willingly agrees to Aslan's
offer of himself in place of Edmund. She mistakenly
believes her moment of victory is at hand.

Similarly, the devil undoubtedly rejoiced at the death
of Jesus, not fully understanding the full plan of
redemption God had decreed. With Jesus' resurrection,
though, sin, death, and Satan are defeated.

**82) After Peter, Susan, and Lucy are brought to meet
Aslan, they prepare for a feast celebrating that
the four thrones of Cair Paravel will be filled.
But we soon read "good times having just begun
were already drawing to an end." What does this
mean?**

As they prepare for the great feast, they experience joy
and peace being with Aslan and seeing the happiness
he has brought to all Narnia. They know that the
power of the White Witch is coming to an end, and
that spring is about to arrive. They do not fully
realize, though, the battle that must be fought—and
the sacrifice Aslan must make—before the final victory
over the Witch can be achieved.

Here we can see a parallel with the earthly life of
Jesus. Right up until His entry into Jerusalem for
Passover, things seemed to be going pretty well. These
were "good times" for His apostles; they did not yet
fully grasp all Jesus needed to suffer, and probably
expected things would only get better. After all, Jesus'

popularity led the people of Jesrusalem to welcome Him with palm branches and shouts of "Hosanna" (see Matthew 21:6-11). Known as a prophet powerful in word and deed, many people had heard His word and would come miles to be in His presence. Not a few of his disciples were more or less hoping for this to continue *ad infinitum*. However, very shortly after the Last Supper, Jesus' passion took place.

83) There seems to be an obvious connection between the Last Supper of Jesus and the great feast with Aslan.

Yes. We can see how the children's feast with Aslan reflects Jesus' Last Supper with His apostles. After sharing a final meal with those who were closest to them, both Jesus and Aslan soon give up their lives and suffer cruel deaths. Both know that they have to sacrifice their lives for the benefit of others.

84) What similarities exist between the suffering, death, and resurrection of Aslan and that of Jesus?

The similarities are striking. They include the following:

- Both willingly lay down their lives to save others. In Aslan's sacrifice, Edmund is spared and Narnia restored; in Jesus' sacrifice, the whole world is saved from sin and death, and the kingdom of heaven is opened to those who accept Him as savior.

- Though both know their deaths are necessary, they are sad and afraid. Much like Jesus' agony in the garden, Aslan on his way to his death is in much agony and pain in the forest and asks his friends to stay with him.

- In their sufferings, both Aslan and Jesus are treated cruelly and unmercifully by their torturers, but neither ever complain, protest, or resist; they willingly accept whatever happens to them.

- Aslan, like Jesus, is careful to make sure that the blow falls on him alone and that his friends are not swept up in the frenzy of his killers and harmed. And, like Jesus, it is women who remain most faithful to Aslan in his darkest hour and beyond.

- Susan and Lucy watch Aslan's sufferings helplessly, knowing that there is nothing they can do. Similarly, Jesus' mother, Mary, and Mary Magdalene watch Christ die on Calvary and know they too can do nothing and that it has to be done.

- Aslan is mocked and ridiculed during his torment, and even endures having a muzzle put on him. This mirrors Jesus' crowning with thorns and the mockery He endured.

- Once the crowd of tormenters departs, the girls approach Aslan's body, take off the muzzle, and wipe away his blood. Here we see a parallel with Jesus being taken down from the Cross, and those who love Him removing the crown of thorns and cleansing His body of the blood.

- Eventually the sky turns gold as the sun rises. Then the girls hear a loud noise as the Stone

Table splits in two. This is reminiscent of the curtain in the Temple being torn in two at the death of Jesus. When the girls go back to the table where Aslan had been lying, he is not there (like Christ not being in the tomb when the stone is removed).

- Susan and Lucy believe Aslan is a ghost until he asks them to touch his mane and they feel the warmth of his breath. This is similar to Jesus' disciples not believing it was Him until they saw and felt His wounds.

85) So *is* Aslan an allegorical representation of Jesus?

Yes and no. As Narnia scholar Andrew Rislen has stated, "Aslan both is and is not Jesus." According to C.S. Lewis himself, Aslan takes the role of a Christ-like figure, though he is *not* an allegorical portrayal of Christ: "If Aslan represented the immaterial Deity, he would be an allegorical figure. In reality, however, he is an invention giving an imaginary answer to the question, 'What might Christ become like if there really were a world like Narnia and He chose to be incarnate and die and rise again in that world as He actually has done in ours?' This is not allegory at all."

CHAPTER 9

AFTER ASLAN'S TRiUmPH

86) Why does the Stone Table crack?

The Stone Table cracks because the conditions are met for "the magic deeper than the Deep Magic." Aslan has sacrificed himself for Edmund, only to rise again to end the reign of the White Witch and bring about peace and justice in Narnia.

Similarly, St. Paul tells us that the Law, having brought us to Christ, no longer has power over us. That does not mean that we are now free to break the law—e.g., murder, rape, and sin to our heart's desire. Rather, it means that the Law was like a tutor whose purpose was to bring us to Christ. Just as grade school is meant to prepare us for high school, and high school for college, and college (we hope) for a successful career, the Law was to prepare us for the guidance of the Holy Spirit, who makes us able to transcend the Law, not break it. Living by the law of love in Christ, we fulfill everything the Moral Law requires.

87) Aslan says to Susan and Lucy that the Witch knew part of the mystery of the Stone Table, but there was a "magic deeper that she did not know." What does this mean?

The Witch, though powerful, is not as powerful as Aslan, who is the creator of Narnia and knowledgeable in the ways of his father, the Emperor. She was not present before the dawn of time and was thus ignorant of "the Deeper Magic." In a similar way, the devil, though powerful as a fallen angel, does not know the mind of God or have a perfect knowledge of His plans.

St. Paul, speaking of both the human and demonic "rulers" who conspired to murder Jesus, declares, "But we impart a secret and hidden wisdom of God, which God decreed before the ages for our glorification. None of the rulers of this age understood this; for if they had, they would not have crucified the Lord of glory" (1 Corinthians 2:7-8).

88) How does the Deeper Magic relate to the Eucharist?

The Deeper Magic is known only to Aslan and his father, the Emperor, and then believed by those who witness its power.

The Eucharist is the most profound miracle God grants us. The sacred consecration of bread and wine becoming the body and blood of Christ was instituted by Jesus, and He shared that with His disciples, who then shared this with the rest of God's people. Only those who have a deep faith can really believe, see, and witness the "deeper magic" of the bread and wine becoming the body and blood of Jesus.

89) Why does Aslan offer himself to be sacrificed?

Aslan tells the girls that if someone is sacrificed in the place of a sinner, then "the Table would crack and death itself would start working backwards." This is a parallel to Jesus' sacrifice on the Cross so that all sinners can have eternal life.

90) What is similar about how Aslan and Jesus both return?

When he comes back to life, Aslan, like Jesus, appears as he was before his brutal torture and death. His broken body is completely healed, and he has the power of immortality about him.

CHAPTER 10

THE GREAT BATTLE

91) What scene in *The Lion, the Witch, and the Wardrobe* represents the power of the Holy Spirit?

When Aslan breathes new life into the statues at the Witch's castle, he does what God did when creating Adam—He "breathed into his nostrils the breath of life, and man became a living being" (Genesis 2:7). He also does what Jesus did in an even more profound way when He breathed on the Apostles and said, "Receive the Holy Spirit" (John 20:22).

After Aslan breathes on all the animals, Lewis describes their restoration to life as looking like a flame as it burns a piece of paper. Except, instead of turning to ash, the stone turns into the animal's flesh. This calls to mind not only the "breath" of the Spirit, but also the tongues of fire that appeared over the heads of the Apostles on Pentecost, the birthday of the Church (see Acts 2:3). The breath of Aslan restores those who were dead to the life of the Holy Spirit. Now that the animals have been restored, Aslan reminds them that their work isn't over yet and that they must find the battle and help defeat the Witch and her army. Similarly, the Christian is called, by his baptism and confirmation, to do battle with the world, the flesh, and the evil.

92) After this, what does Aslan command that Jesus also constantly tells us we must also do?

Aslan makes sure that all of the animals take care of each other and use their strength to that end. In short, he commands them to love one another as he has loved them (see John 15:17). He makes sure that those who can't keep up (the children, dwarfs, and small animals) are riding on those who can run quickly and are strong (centaurs, unicorns, horses, giants, and eagles). Aslan uses the natural talent of the lions and dogs (that is, their smell) to help them locate the battle.

Jesus calls on us to do the same thing. We who are strong and materially blessed have a duty to protect the weak and the poor, those who cannot take care of themselves—the unborn, the disabled, the dying. We are also called to use the gifts God has given us to better the kingdom of God on Earth (see 1 Corinthians 12:4-27)

CHAPTER II

AFTER THE BATTLE

93) Tell me the meaning behind the magical cordial that Father Christmas gives to Lucy.

The cordial Lucy has been given reminds us of the sacramental power of holy water and the healing and sanctifying power of baptism. It is supposed to have great healing powers, and was given to her by Father Christmas, as holy water is blessed by priests, who act *in persona Christi* on earth. The cordial is reminiscent of Jesus' words: "Whoever drinks of the water that I shall give him will never thirst; the water that I shall give him will become in him a spring of water welling up to eternal life" (John 4:13-14).

94) Why does Aslan rebuke Lucy?

Because Lucy lingers over Edmund when her duty is to help everyone who has been hurt in the battle. Aslan asks, "Must *more* people die for Edmund?" in part to remind her of the suffering he has endured already for Edmund, but also to remind her that her responsibility extends beyond her immediate family. The rebuke is stern, but loving. For it is aimed at reminding her that she is a Queen and that her responsibility is for the whole realm of Narnia. In the same way, Jesus reminds us that we are not simply to love those who love us, nor to care only for our immediate relatives and friends, but that our call is to love our neighbor— that is, anyone we meet.

95) Edmund's appearance changes throughout *The Lion, the Witch and the Wardrobe*. Is this connected with his actions?

Yes, this seems to be the case. We can see this at various points in the story. On their way back home after their first adventure together in Narnia, Lucy asks Edmund if he feels OK because he doesn't look well. This is after he has eaten the Turkish Delight and decided to turn his siblings over to the White Witch. He replies, "I am alright," but it seems clear that evil is affecting his appearance. By contrast, at the end of the story, after his talk with Aslan and being healed from the great battle by the special potion Father Christmas gave to Lucy, the others comment on how well he looks again. By being converted to the good, Edmund has healed from his physical wounds and from the evil that he has allowed to overtake him.

Ultimately, it is Aslan's sacrifice of his very life that saves Edmund from the consequences of his sin and restores him to health. Lucy wants to tell Edmund all about what Aslan did for him, but Susan convinces her how awful it would be for him to know. As Christians, we know the total sacrifice that Jesus made for us on the Cross, yet we continue to sin. Out of love for us, Jesus suffered and died in a way that we could not imagine enduring—to save us from our sins and give us eternal life.

96) **How does Aslan provide food for everyone the day after the battle?**

He provides the food through working a miracle. This event bears a striking similarity to Jesus' feeding of the 5,000 by multiplying five loaves and two fish (see Mark 6:35-44).

97) **Why does the White Stag appear at the end of the story?**

The White Stag appears at the end of the book to lead the four children—now the four rulers of Narnia—home to our world, but only if they freely choose to follow him.

In a similar way, Jesus is the Good Shepherd who will lead us if we choose to follow Him willingly. He became man and died for us so that we would join Him in eternal life.

The white stag is a medieval symbol of Christ. In other words, this is another appearance of Aslan "in disguise." It is he who leads the children back to our world because he is, in fact, the Lord of both Narnia and our world. While trying to follow the White Stag, the four children are led back to the lamppost and Wardrobe door, back to their home.

98) **What symbolism is associated with a stag in European mythology?**

The stag is symbol of Christ. A white stag is also a familiar creature in Celtic and northern European myths and legends. Its appearance is an indicator of the near presence of the "Otherworld." In this case, the White Stag leads the children back to their world.

When all four of them have followed the White Stag to the lamp-post, they don't know that their world and home lie just beyond. None of the four fully remembers the lamp-post. They are not aware that the Wardrobe—and their old lives—lies right ahead of them.

99) At the end of the book, what does the Professor mean when he says, "I don't think it would be any good trying to go back through the wardrobe door to get the coats…no, you won't get there by that route. Indeed, don't try to get there at all. It will happen when you are not looking for it…keep your eyes open." What does he mean by this?

The very nature of Narnia and its connection with our world makes it impossible to go back to it the same way. In fact, the children should not even seek to go back, as the Professor tells them. Rather, when Narnia needs them, it will call to them and lead them back in.

We cannot look force open a door to heaven; we cannot find our own way there. We cannot *make* Grace happen by our will power. We cannot force God's hand or put Him in our debt. As Jesus puts it, "You did not choose me. I chose you" (John 15:16). God promises us that He desires us to come to Him and to know Him. But this must happen according to His will, not ours. We have been given insights as to what heaven is like (for example, in the Holy Eucharist, marriage, children) but to find the way to heaven, we must keep our eyes on God and living a Christian life. If we do this, God will call us there in His good time.

100) What happens to Peter, Susan, Edmund and Lucy when they pass through the Wardrobe back into our world?

They find that, despite the fact that they have lived for years in Narnia and grown to adulthood there, when they return to our world, no time at all has passed and they are again the ages they were when they entered the Wardrobe. This recalls the fact that "with the Lord one day is as a thousand years, and a thousand years as one day" (2 Peter 3:8). It also reminds us that children can be far wiser than adults because of their hearts being open to God. As Jesus says, "Truly, I say to you, whoever does not receive the kingdom of God like a child shall not enter it" (Mark 10:15).

ACKNOWLEDGMENTS

The following authors contributed to this book
(listed alphabetically):

Sue Allen
Tom Allen
Tommy Allen
Jennifer Cope
Michael Flickinger
Sara McLaughlin
Matthew Pinto
Mark Shea

Editorial and technical assistance by Michael Fontecchio, Michael J. Miller, and Thomas A. Szyszkiewicz. Cover design by Devin Schadt. Marketing and public relations coordinated by Maximus Media Group and Christopher Cope.

NARNIA
OUTREACH

—NarniaOutreach.com—

Join **Narnia Outreach** in our promotion of the epic adventure, *The Chronicles of Narnia: The Lion, the Witch and the Wardrobe*. Destined to become a timeless classic, *Narnia* is a grand-scale, live-action movie that combines the grandeur of *Lord of the Rings* with the fantasy and virtue of *The Wizard of Oz*. A classic story of "good versus evil," *Narnia* is a film that will be loved and seen by millions. The adventure begins on **December 9, 2005**.

You can play a role in bringing home this wonderful film's inspiring message. **NarniaOutreach.com,** an initiative of Catholic Outreach, is a fan site and resource center for parishes, schools, groups who want to use the film as a faith-formation opportunity. Learn more about the movie, view trailers, check out FAQs, learn how to start a study group, download free study guides, order Narnia-related materials, and much more! Help spread C.S. Lewis' message of inspiration and hope to your parish, family, and friends.

Also available at NarniaOutreach.com: Before you embark on your adventure, order copies of the definitive Narnia "travel guide": *A Guide to Narnia—100 Questions about The Chronicles of Narnia: The Lion, the Witch and the Wardrobe*. Written by the editors of Catholic Exchange, this book will take you deeper into the story and help you understand the Christian symbolism found throughout this classic tale.

Three <u>Free</u> Study Guides

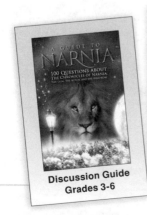

Discussion Guide
Grades 3-6

Discussion Guide
Grades 7-12

Adult Faith Formation
Study Guide

A GUIDE TO
NARNIA

100 QUESTIONS ABOUT THE CHRONICLES OF NARNIA:
THE LION, THE WITCH & THE WARDROBE

On December 9th, millions will enter the world of Narnia. This is a world full of intrigue and wonder, created in the mind of the great Christian author C.S. Lewis. Beneath the surface of the story lies a beautiful metaphorical tale of Jesus Christ and God's plan for humanity. Learn the true meaning of this classic tale, share it with your family, friends, students and parishioners, and your movie-going experience will surpass mere entertainment, becoming a life-lesson on the Catholic Faith.

This is the perfect resource for individuals, schools, and parishes who wish to pass on the life-changing lessons that can be learned in this epic film.

Bulk Discounts Available!
Retail Price $6.95

Call **800-376-0520** for details or order online at www.ascensionpress.com

---

❐ Yes, please send me copies of *A Guide to Narnia*

Send me _____ booklets x _____ ea = $ _____

Shipping = $ _____

Total = $ _____

❐ Cash   ❐ Check   ❐ Credit Card

Shipping/Handling Rates:
1-9 . . . . $5
10-24 . . . . $7
25-49 . . . . $11
50-99 . . . . $13
100+ actual shipping charges apply
Please call for actual charges

Please make checks payable to: Ascension Press
W5180 Jefferson St., Necedah, WI 54646
Tel: 800-376-0520   E-mail: sales@ascensionpress.com

Bill to Name _____

Address _____

City _____ State ____ Zip _____

Phone _____ Fax _____

E-mail _____

Card #: _____

MC ❐ Visa ❐ Discover ❐ Exp. Date: _____
                                    (required!)

Ship to Name _____

Address _____

City _____ State ____ Zip _____

Phone _____ Fax _____

Keep *your passion* for Christ alive by learning the Bible with Catholic Scripture Study.

Catholic Scripture Study (CSS), written by leading Catholic Scripture scholars Scott Hahn and Mark Shea and long available on CatholicExchange.com, is now available in a Group Study Program. Launched in 2003, participating groups around the country and overseas are raving about this powerful, life-changing Bible Study.

In addition to the in-depth and solidly Catholic Bible study and commentaries, CSS now offers a popular classroom format that fosters real learning and true Christian fellowship. Catholics no longer have to stray from the Church to find a vibrant Bible Study!

For more information, please email us:
info@CatholicScriptureStudy.com

or visit:
www.CatholicScriptureStudy.com

Catholic Scripture Study

LEARN MORE ABOUT THE CHRISTIAN SYMBOLISM FOUND IN THE LION, THE WITCH AND THE WARDROBE

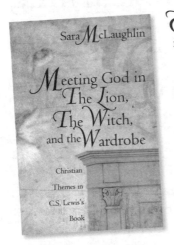

*E*nhance your enjoyment of *The Lion, the Witch and the Wardrobe* with this indispensable guide to understanding the Christian themes in C.S. Lewis's timeless classic. See how imagination becomes reality as God's Word comes to life. As a bonus, the preface includes surprising and humorous anedotes about C.S. Lewis, friend and professor. Author Sara McLaughlin takes you on a fascinating journey behind the scenes of the first book in *The Chronicles of Narnia*, now a major motion picture.

Ordering Information

Bookstores can order through distributors Spring Arbor or Ingram, or directly from the publisher. Please call 1-877-421-7327 or visit pleasantwordbooks.com. Also available at amazon.com or barnesandnoble.com. ISBN 1-4141-0442-1.

About the Author

Sara McLaughlin, author of *Meeting God in the Lion, the Witch and the Wardrobe* (Pleasant Word, 2005), is an instructor of English at Texas Tech University. She regularly teaches workshops and has published numerous articles about the life and work of C.S. Lewis. Her book, *Meeting God in Silence* (Tyndale, 1993), was endorsed by Walter Hooper, who served as Lewis' personal secretary. McLaughlin is a contributing editor for *The Lamp-Post*, the official journal of the Southern California C. S. Lewis Society. She can be contacted at sara.mclaughlin@ttu.edu

Life is Short.
Support Good Media.

The **American Family Film Foundation (AFFF)** was founded to address the problem of the erosive influence of the media on youth and families. AFFF is a unique non-profit organization dedicated to the development and support of popular entertainment that is positive and enlightening.

We accomplish this goal by offering media that communicates our positive message. The Foundation serves as collaborator or producer on media projects that communicate our special niche. AFFF directly or indirectly helps realize projects of all sizes and ambitions – from websites to 30-second spots to video programs to full-length feature films. We also offer media consultation and production assistance to non-profits looking to effectively communicate their messages.

AFFF's team of professionals work in development, production, post-production, promotion and the business side of the media industry. Our expertise enables us to create high-quality productions at a significantly reduced cost for distribution to schools, families, social service organizations, and community groups throughout the country.

We rely on your support to help us accomplish our mission. Please make a tax-deductible donation to us online at www.afff.tv or mail your tax-deductible donation to us at:

AFFF
PO Box 231664
Encinitas, CA 92023

Thank you.

www.afff.tv